mindscaping

design your future

mindscaping

design your future

Stephanie Churchill

Thorsons
An Imprint of HarperCollins*Publishers*
77 – 85 Fulham Palace Road,
Hammersmith, London W6 8JB

The Thorsons website address is:
www.thorsons.com

Published by Thorsons 2000

10 9 8 7 6 5 4 3 2 1

A catalogue record for this book
is available from the British Library

ISBN 0 7225 3959 2

Printed and bound in Great Britain by
Caledonian International Book
Manufacturing Ltd, Glasgow

For John, Gratia and Julia

acknowledgments

This book was made possible by the support and encouragement of many. Without them it would not have come about. A great number of ideas have come from others one way or another, one idea leading to the next. I would like to express my gratitude to all those whose paths I have crossed, who have taught me and enriched my life.

In particular I would like to thank:

Eileen Campbell at HarperCollins for her vision that a talk could become a book.

Belinda Budge at Thorsons, whose advice, optimism and belief steered me (a first time author) as I struggled to make sense of things.

Judy Chilcote, my agent, for her good care.

Ann Rafter for giving me the time and space to write this book.

Mary-Louise Montgomery, who alongside her regular work helped with all the drafts.

Martyn Holmes for his research and suggestions.

Julie Thorne for her assistance with producing the first talk.

Claudia Turske for valuable advice and help in the editing of the manuscript.

Daniella Sieff for her useful comments and ideas.

Angela Bernstein for her belief and encouragement.

Sonny Herman, Jonathan Rutherfurd Best, **David Gill** and **Andy Freitag-Loringhoven** for sharing with me their specialist knowledge.

Everyone who has been part of the many focus groups.

My daughter Julia whose treasured concern and editing expertise helped me through the last weeks, and **Gratia** for being an inspiration to us all.

All at **Stephanie Churchill PR** for their enthusiasm, research and support.

The children who shared their future with me, including the girls of **Francis Holland School**.

Everyone at Thorsons for their help and energy.

The single most important contributor was my son John. He was an active partner, discussing through concepts and encouraging me to re-think topics. His invaluable insight and knowledge made a great contribution and in a way this book is his as well as mine.

contents

What is mindscaping? 11
Introduction 15
Integration 19

ourselves

energy 25
relationship 31
selfcare 37
personalhealth 41
spendingsaving 45
time 49
sensorydynamics 53
voluntarysimplicity 57
freetime 61
sexuality 67
beyourself 71
curiosity 75
genderfusion 79
birthdeath 83

our work

work2000+ 91
individuality 101
caringconsumer 105
productappeal 109
shopping 113
money 117
englishlanguage 123
awareness 127

our society

arttransforms 133
newtradition 137
livingwithnature 141
youngageoldage 145
protection 149
fooddrink 151
integralmedicine 157
technology 163
habitats 171
socialmigration 179
population 183
parenting 185
education 189
lifelearning 195
ethics 197
divinediscontent 201
oneplanet 205

conclusion 209
suggested reading 218
index 222

what is mindscaping?

mindscape /'mʌIn(d)skeIp/*n. & v.* • *n.* 1 conceptual landscape of the imagination. 2 a mental diagram of plans and aspirations. • *v.* 3 the process of evolving a personal scheme or model (of a thing or condition not yet existing). 4 contemplate, plan, or conceive, esp. towards desirable future events.

Mindscaping creates a landscape of the future in your mind. Envisioning how life might be. BY UNDERSTANDING THE NEW CURRENTS DESCRIBED IN THIS BOOK YOU CAN EXAMINE YOUR LIFE AND DECIDE WHETHER YOU NEED TO MAKE CHANGES.

Mindscaping is roaming in your mind, playing with different scenarios. Blending ideas, assimilating, crystallizing, questioning and ultimately constructing a new framework for yourself or your company. Imagine yourself, your life, your work and the products and services that would make up this new world.

Leave behind the way things are now. Only look ahead at what the possibilities can be. How would you really like them to be? You will discover avenues you had never thought of before. Entire new scenarios that seem so obvious, but that you just had not reached out to.

Never mindscape in your office or sitting behind a desk. It does not work. Do it outside the habitual. Go to another place. Mindscape in in-between places: the car, plane, train, or when walking or quietly at home. It can be done alone or with a partner, friend or colleague. In a group it works if everyone is equal, no scoring of ideas, no one forcing their view. That blocks the process. Take your time, an afternoon or evening. Usually the best ideas come towards the end.

Use the information in this book to form a background, the scenery. Use your own and each others' ideas, resources, understanding, knowledge and creativity to construct new shapes, blocks, buildings, formats, ways of doing things. Consider the new thinking that will run through all aspects of our lives and superimpose the emerging scenery. See if it fits against the background of the future. Adapt it if necessary.

Once you have created a picture of the future, consider how to bridge the gap between the present and the future. What steps need to be taken? Examine all the practical elements. Construct a concrete plan of how to achieve this.

MINDSCAPING CREATES SPACE FOR THE NEW. IT GIVES AN OPPORTUNITY TO RETHINK HOW YOU ARE LIVING AND WORKING. It helps to assess whether changes need to be made and introduces new opportunities. Mindscaping is a spontaneous fusing of ideas. In fact this book is mindscaped. Mindscaping is easy. It should flow. It's fun.

introduction

the future is here It is unfolding around us yet most of us are not aware of its messages. **Our mind-set causes us to automatically focus on what we know.** We create a routine life for ourselves: the same job, friends, books, newspapers, restaurants, holidays, blocking the space for new ideas.

In my work it is necessary to landscape the future so that my company can develop images for brands that connect with the time ahead. I am curious about how people live, eat, work, think, spend their free time. Why do they buy certain products and not others? I look for cutting edge thinking in design, art, music, journalism, food, religion and medicine. I study best sellers, film grossers, market research data, lectures and think-tank information. Talk to children and young people about how they see the future. Join in discussion groups, travel and interact with a diverse mix of open-minded individuals.

After absorbing this information, patterns and trends emerge. Sometimes a trend is based on hard fact, often it starts with a 'feel', a hunch that slowly takes hold. Usually the same indications come from different places, and I assimilate and then synchronize them. Gradually a picture of a trend emerges. I would like to share these trends with you. Once you get to know these new directions their manifestations become apparent. The same messages are conveyed in articles, books, art, music. SO THE FUTURE IS HERE AND WE CAN SEE IT.

We can have the freedom to choose our future, and to make a choice that is balanced and well-informed. THIS BOOK IS A TOOL TO STIMULATE, INFORM AND CHALLENGE. To help create the future, adapt to the future and prepare to cope with the consequences of change. I am fully aware of the enormous amount of environmental, economic and social uncertainties we are facing. However, I have decided to concentrate more on the positive developments of the future.

This book is not about predictions. The future is unproven territory. This book is about what might happen and what is already happening. It is by no means certain that all the trends mentioned will occur. Every trend has a counter trend. In order for a coherent picture to emerge I have made choices. In the end it is my vision and that of other well-informed people. Hopefully thought-provoking and no doubt not always right.

To me it is not important to be right, and although I have written it as if everything will happen, **MY INTENTION IS TO DEVELOP AN AWARENESS ABOUT THE FUTURE,** imagining, speculating and anticipating the possibilities of time ahead. I have realized, after giving talks on mindscaping, that **DISCUSSING THE FUTURE INSPIRES THE PRESENT.** That somehow it frees up the mind to create space for the new.

What is the best way to read this book? I recommend that you read it once through, beginning to end. This should take you an hour or so. At a later date, when you are thinking about a particular issue, re-read any relevant topics. With a different focus we have different eyes.

integration

whole systems Integration runs through all aspects of our lives, from the environment and commerce to health and psychology. To embrace this way of thinking requires a fundamental change in mindset, the paradigm through which we view the world. Essentially, the message is simple: integration sees the connection, depth and interdependency of all parts. **Integration is a response to new thinking with values that reflect our needs.**

We can no longer separate our body, emotions, mind and soul. Connecting the different parts of our internal and external worlds leads to greater fulfilment of the individual, the company and the whole.

Integration acknowledges the fundamental laws of nature and change. In understanding these principles and putting them into practice, we no longer work against the natural law.

isolation and constant competition
are replaced with
assimilation, fusion
and synergy

Each part helps the other, creating a stronger relationship based on a deeper integrity. The whole is greater than the sum of its parts.

We want to live whole, satisfying, integrated lives, where work and play naturally complement each other. To live in balance, we need to allow our personal and commercial spheres to be 'integrated', to allow for change, creativity and connection. Such a change in mindset is far from idealistic. Integration is practical. We can apply this understanding to our daily lives, our health, relationships, businesses, products and social structures. Creating a future where we want to live.

design
your
future

ourselves

energy

energy is everything The world view expressed in our present culture is that we live in an inert world, a world of things and objects, a Newtonian dream where everything is a grand machine, from the spinning universe to the human body. Like a machine everything eventually just falls apart and breaks. Our society reflects the scientific view of the 18th and 19th centuries. We have not yet caught up with ourselves.

The world that 20th century physicists have discovered is alive: everything is energy. Solid matter is just frozen light waiting to be freed to change its form and manifest itself as something else.

Energy is what gives us life. We receive it from the sun, from the air, the food we eat, the people we love. There is a constant exchange of energy flowing through the interdependent web of life.

energy is the real currency

When we meet a person, whether we are aware of it or not, we sense their energy. Is it compatible with ours? Does it harmonize with or disturb the frequency that we feel comfortable with? Whether we believe in 'vibes' or not we can feel them. Just sense what happens when we walk into a room. We feel something. We feel energy.

the language of energy

Energy has a language – it expresses itself. Just as scientists develop languages to describe the transformations of energy, so can we. We can feel the quantity of our energy: Are our 'fuel tanks' empty or full? Does the quality of our energy feel harmonious or disturbed? Can we allow our energy to flow from one thing to another, does it jump about, or does it get stuck somewhere?

How efficient are we? Do we conserve our energy or do we burn it all away?

energy is precious

The way that we live today can drain us of energy. In developing our personal language around energy we can advance discussion and encourage awareness. Investigate how you might improve your energy and bring balance to the present system. More energy in our lives gives us the capacity for more love, more creativity, more life.

energy cultivation

Ancient cultures and civilizations explored the science of energy. They lived by the wisdom of traditional teachings that passed on the knowledge of energy. They learnt to enhance their energy through meditation, breathing, singing, movement and dancing. They knew about the energy of food and herbs. Two traditions of energy cultivation that are becoming part of our culture are Indian yoga and Chinese chi kung. These traditions teach practices designed to harmonize and develop the life force known as qi/chi in China and as prana in India.

In January 1995 BUSINESS WEEK magazine reported that in Japan senior executives of major companies such Sony, Mitsubishi Electric, NEC and Casio computers were training with chi kung masters. Sony Corporation has a research team studying chi, while ten major companies are funding research at Tokyo's University of Electro-Communications. At the governmental level, Japan's ministry of International Trade and Industry has formed a committee to look into the practical uses of chi energy.

The NHS has allocated funds for hospitals to employ feng shui experts to review the interiors of hospital wards, waiting rooms and accident and emergency departments.

energy application

We are beginning to see the reintroduction of energetic principles into our modern culture. Medicine is being influenced by treatments such as homeopathy, acupuncture and ayurveda, all of which are based on an energetic understanding of man and disease. ArCHItecture is investigating and integrating the ancient principles of geomancy (known in the East as feng shui and vastu shastra), the science of energetic flow through the landscape and within buildings. We are seeing corporate headquarters and family homes built on the sacred geometry of energy currents. Energy is being integrated into every art from constitutional cooking to therapeutic music. By bringing energy back into our culture we create ways of living that respect the flow of life.

energy +
creativity =
innovation

relationship

it is all a relationship Our world is becoming increasingly interconnected. Financial swings on the stock market, environmental disruptions and conflict on the other side of the world can influence what is happening in our home country. We are interdependent.

we
are
interconnected

Whatever we do, however we live, we are drawn into relationships. The primary relationships for many of us are between ourselves, our family and friends. We want to enjoy our relationships more, to learn to enrich the intimacy and communication between ourselves. In our relationships with people, the natural world and even possessions, we want to be connected, to feel that we are part of a bigger picture.

new forms

Personal relationships can take many forms. It is increasingly seen as normal for men and women to live alone and have fulfiling lives. Women are realizing that they have a choice as to whether they want to be mothers. Life has so much to offer and parenting is a huge responsibility. The traditional structure of marriage is under threat. In the past, marriage was set and formal, today, husband and wife have the opportunity to redefine roles. Whilst marriage will remain a choice, 'not-for-life partnerships' is an option allowing couples to experience a committed relationship without the 'life sentence' of marriage. It is becoming socially acceptable for gay people to form marriages, and the possibility of gay families is developing. An age gap between partners is less of a cause for concern. We are learning to accept other people's needs and freedom.

In May 1999 the Canadian Supreme Court ruled that it is unconstitutional that the term 'spouse' applies only to heterosexual couples. This ruling stopped short of giving legal recognition to gay marriages, but some Canadian legal experts believe such steps could follow. In Europe registered gay partnership laws have been passed in Denmark, Norway, Iceland, Sweden, Greenland and the Netherlands.

householding

The 20th century has seen the deterioration of the extended family, leaving us with the isolated nuclear family. Now people are realizing how much support family can offer, and coming to see that in order to survive in a society that does not offer much support we need to rethink the role of the family. The family is the first unit of society: trouble in the family creates trouble in society.

we are seeing new options

Due to the combination of insufficient pension provisions. Multi-generational kinship units and working parents and clans are developing. *CLANNING* is creating a family of like-minded people. Don't imagine it is just for hippies! *CLANNING* is smart and trendy – for professionals, artists and families. Our friends are becoming our family, participating in clanningchildcare and providing a support system. Increasingly such clans are choosing to live together in the same building, complex or street.

friends
are
family

selfcare

valuing who we are Most of us can acknowledge that we don't look after ourselves as much as we would like. We find it difficult to feel our intrinsic self-worth and value. Is it easier for us to believe in original sin than the basic goodness of being human? As the demands of our lives increase, we are challenging that limiting belief.

**we are finding that it is
more important to live balanced lives
than to chase material success**

We are gradually realizing that the source and quality of our experience is ourself. We are becoming interested in the actualization of our potential. We are valuing who we are, seeing that how we eat, feel, look and think can all influence our experience of life.

practical selfcare

What is selfcare? Is it about self-centredness? Far from it. When we feel good we can give the world and those around us more. Selfcare is about putting back into ourselves what life has taken out. Giving ourselves the resources to keep growing and enjoying our lives. When we experience stress at work and in our relationships, we can take the time to invest in a massage, take a walk in the countryside or read a new book by our favourite author. When we are moving through an emotional problem, we go to see a therapist. We are beginning to learn how to support ourselves and to realize that we need not feel guilty or weird for doing so. We are starting to create support teams of personal health advisers, body workers, personal development consultants and therapists. All these professionals are people who can help us resource ourselves.

personalhealth

our responsibility We have grown up in a dependence culture, relying on our health needs being met by professional doctors and a huge pharmaceutical industry. When something goes wrong we go to the doctor, just as we go to the mechanic when our car breaks down. Although our medical system has given us the ability to cure many serious ailments, the professionalism of the system has also disempowered us, leaving us unable to take care of our own health.

Our health is in the hands of a structure that is only designed to work with sickness, not maintain health. The only time we see a doctor is when something is wrong. More of us are taking matters into our own hands, realizing that we can prevent sickness by strengthening our immune systems, improving digestion, learning how to eat and exercising correctly. There are simple ways to support ourselves, such as eating organic food and taking vitamins or herbs. We all need to learn how to deal with stress. Stress releases hormones that, when accumulated, cause toxicity that knocks out our immune system and makes us more susceptible to disease and ageing.

Making our health our personal responsibility is not about avoiding doctors, but about empowering ourselves to take charge of our own well-being. Before long we will be able to self-diagnose through internet medical services: visits to the doctor will be reserved for more serious complaints.

the health industry

Scientific research is being carried out into health and wellness. This research will lead to the development of new products, diets and ways of living. Insurance companies are beginning to realize that prevention is financially viable: the healthier we are, the less they have to pay out. Staying healthy makes sense.

Exercise boosts the immune system. Exercise science can now help us to exercise the whole body: build muscle, develop flexibility and increase our aerobic and anaerobic capacity. Depending on our age, time and willingness we can develop a personal health and exercise programme specific to our needs. As research continues into the area of human longevity, we are going to learn that we have the choice to lengthen and improve the quality of our lives. We are going to be able to live longer, healthier and stronger.

the softer experience

We are also learning that exercise does not just have to be about sweat and muscle. We don't have to be out in the park jogging every day. Healthy exercise can also be soft and internal. We can go for a long walk, breathe, do yoga, t'ai chi, pilates or other gentle movement practices. These forms of exercise help us to relax and keep us flexible, strong and mentally sharp.

spendsaving

the skill of consuming Our culture is based on capitalist economics, emphasizing the importance of personal financial independence. We all want economic freedom so that we can buy what we want. The world we live in is changing and we can see the effects of blind capitalist progress on our environment and health. As a result we are becoming more cautious about how we spend our money. We are thinking about sustainability, being economical and enjoying spending the minimum for the maximum.

spending

If we are creative we can find other options: borrowing, bartering and leasing. We need to embrace other forms of economic expression.

alternative financial choices are as much about self-empowerment and psychological benefit as they are about fiscal sense

saving

The job market is looking more insecure. Whilst in the past a job was for life, today it is looking likely that many of us will work to temporary contracts. Saving for economic independence is becoming even more important. We need to save for things that we really want and to give us security when we may not be able to find work. Where do we actually save our money? What is our money doing when invested? These are questions that many of us are beginning to ask. We want to be able to bank and make investments that support the planet and our personal values.

safespending

time

time design Our world is speeding up. The speed of transportation, communication, service and transaction is accelerating. Companies can now operate at the speed of digital thought. This acceleration will inevitably lead to complexity and stress. Traditional structures are being challenged by progress, as businesses become seven-day, 24-hour operations.

Many companies are deciding to out-source. To save time by contracting certain tasks to outside specialists. What could we *out-source* in our working lives that would save us time and give us the opportunity to concentrate on more important things?

The demands that our lives place on us mean that we need to be more creative with the time that is at our disposal. We want to be able to fit everything in, work and play.

Time is relative. Although it can be measured on a watch, when we experience an hour it can pass in a flash or drag on and on. How do we give ourselves the opportunity to make time work for us? As things speed up we need to slow down, to be able to remain in the present and not get caught speeding on our over-used nervous system. We are going to have to develop greater personal discipline to keep ourselves focused. We can either lose ourselves, becoming machines in a demanding commercial system, or we can use these developments to discover flexibility in time management. We can be more creative with our time, we don't have to limit ourselves. We have an opportunity ***TO MAKE TIME WORK FOR US,*** and so to be able to ***'MAKE IT'***.

sharing

The modern mythology of economic independence and progress emphasizes the importance of 'making it'. Surrendering our own agendas allows us to work together with colleagues, family, friends and neighbours. Time sharing becomes an efficient, cost effective and community-building practice. We can share our time and talent: 'I will trade you an hour of my skill for an hour of yours'; possessions, vegetable gardens, cars or tools.

It is not about giving everything away, but about realizing that our society has created a tendency for us to live in small, isolated worlds. We can come together and share, offering each other opportunities and resources that we would not have the time or money to access otherwise.

sensory dynamics

healing through the senses It has been discovered that astronauts feel discomfort in space due to the lack of smells. NASA designers had to add artificial smells to give the instinctual brain necessary reassurance. Sensory impressions are the essence of our experience. We meet the outside world through our sight, smell, taste, touch and hearing. These perceptual channels lead into our brain, stimulating chemical reactions.

Although our senses are subtle, they are also a potent vehicle for healing and we should make use of these tools, allowing our senses to help relax, stimulate and balance.

SMELL has the power to evoke memories and changes in our emotional state. We have been using smell for thousands of years. The ancient inhabitants of Europe, America, India, Egypt and other civilizations used the power of smell for healing and religious ritual. Today in France aromatherapy is prescribed by medical doctors. Experiment with smells and see how they can transform the atmosphere of a room and alleviate a mood. Design the smell for your house to be fresh, welcoming and uplifting.

We can use **SIGHT** by being more aware of the psychological influence of colour. Each colour of the spectrum evokes a particular response within us. If we prefer to wear a particular colour of clothing, it is likely that we are unconsciously trying to balance ourselves. Red energizes, blue stimulates communication and balances thought, green is harmonizing, white calms. Try a different colour, and see how you feel. Next time you see a green field or pass a red flower, consciously let that colour in.

your senses can nourish you

HEARING has always been a powerful transformative tool. In China, India and ancient Greece, musical systems of healing were developed. Sounds stimulate the brain and energy system and can take us on journeys within. They can relax, excite, uplift, soothe and energize, touching our most unreachable places.

The skin is part of the nervous system and the largest organ of the human body. **TOUCH** is healing. It brings us out of the mind and into the present experience of the body. Everything we touch during the day influences us, from the touch of somebody we love to the sensation of concrete under our feet. Different textures surround us with different sensory experiences. From shiny wooden floors, crisp cotton sheets and coarse coir matting, to soft, sensual velvets. Our bodies like to touch natural textiles. The glass and chrome of modern living can make us feel out of touch.

In the East it is understood that specific **TASTES** influence specific tissues and organs and create certain emotional responses. We can alter our mood through food. The sweet taste of love, the spice of enthusiasm and the assertive sour.

voluntary simplicity

speed and stress We exist in a haze of speed, noise and pollution. The demands of modern living put us under enormous stress and uncertainty. There is so much to do, so much sensory stimulation around us. Despite computers and electronic communication we appear to have less and less time. Instead of making life easier for ourselves, we find we are caught up in a habitual and mechanical way of living.

questioning values

voluntary simplicity antidotes a wired culture

We are questioning our beliefs. Asking what it is that gives quality to life. Is it the number of consumer products we have, or is it a simpler, more internal experience? Does the one reflect the other? Voluntary simplicity is a cultural movement slowly gathering influence. The quest for what is essential in our lives.

quality not quantity

The joy of simplicity is already reflected in society. We are discovering we can eat less (oriental influence), own less (zenification of interior design), buy less and enjoy it more. We want quality and integrity, not quantity or luxury.

real goods

freetime

plan for it With less freetime due to work and other responsibilities we need to be more disciplined so that we have the opportunity to do everything that we need and want. With forethought we can turn transitional time into freetime: enjoying a walk to work if possible, taking a book or a pad to write when we know we might have to wait. By adding small things to our day, customizing our work space with music and objects of personal value, we give ourselves a sense of freedom.

the experience

The experience is competing with consumables. Many of us are tired of recreational shopping. We are looking for experiences that add to our lives and skills. Extreme sports, outward bound adventures, travel, visiting new places, learning new skills. We want to learn and grow. We want to spend our money cultivating new and unexplored parts of ourselves. Whether the experience is an adventurous, educational or spiritual one we want it to change our lives. Climbing a mountain, taking night classes in a foreign language, or learning to play a musical instrument.

communing

We see the emergence of THE THIRD PLACE, away from home and work. A comfortable place where we come together to eat, drink or just be. Festivals, eating establishments or community events, such as local performing arts, provide a meeting point.

at home

At home cooking is a pleasure. Cooking for family and friends. Taking time to experiment with ethnic ingredients from different parts of the world.

eating as an event

Planning and tending to our gardens. Investing in our personal plot of nature.

The DIY spirit is growing, even if we can afford to pay for someone else to do it. Learning the skills and gaining satisfaction from this. If we don't do it ourselves, knowing how things should be done. The DIY industry is responding by providing informative leaflets, expert staff, in-store demonstrations and computerized design systems to plan the layout of rooms in your home.

The world is accessible at home through our electronic resource centre. We surf the net for information and we participate in interactive TV and film. EDUTAINMENT Teaching us while we are being entertained.

holidays

Long haul for short stay holidays. Perhaps one week in Eastern Europe, North Africa, Vietnam or Peru. With cheaper and faster air travel this becomes an option. The return of the traveller: staying in small local inns, getting to know places, the people. More of us are interested in exploring eco-tourism: respecting the environment and travelling with a conscience.

the inner life

Freetime is time to care for the soul. For some that is in the form of service and teaching. For others it is more of an internal process: taking time for a contemplative retreat or psychotherapy. We need time for inner growth, for our own cultivation and development. Artistic expression: drawing, painting, writing and sculpting are powerful resources to explore our undiscovered potential.

holidays
or
holydays?

sexuality

anything goes We are living in a time of phone and cyber sex. We face increasingly explicit information and images through the media, internet and film. With so much excess we have become desensitized, and sexual sensationalism has to increase in order to sustain our attention. This is leading to an openness regarding sexual options: age gap, same sex, bisexuality, heterosexuality.

Many of us have suffered from a lack of sexual education, cultural imprinting from our childhood or from the traditional religious relationship to sexuality. As we question, a new understanding is emerging, leading to a more thoughtful approach. Is innocence (purity) and spontaneity the ultimate eroticism? Is the natural language of sexuality more erotic than rehearsed posturing and scripted role playing? We are starting to appreciate that sex is an individual experience and each of us experiences it in a different way.

Since the rise of AIDS we are more thoughtful about entering a sexual relationship, more ready to give it commitment and time. It is seen as more of an accomplishment to have a long-term relationship than a one night stand.

Our sexuality tells our story.
It tells us about our creativity,
energy and trust.

beyourself

as you are Fashion no longer dictates what we can or cannot wear. More of us are tired of conforming and fitting in. We are seeing a slow breakdown in the traditional forms of dressing. Boundaries have been pushed ahead by the gay movement and music stars. We are also reacting against mass consumerism: the instant copying of designer trends in the high street. **We don't all want to look the same.**

Fashion has responded with not just one look for the season, but a multitude. We can wear what feels comfortable and looks good to us, co-ordinating our own style, mixing quality design with basics. We are able to go where we want and not have to dress according to the codes and expectations of others. Just choosing to follow our heart, whether that is exotic or functional. Depending on our day or mood we can have completely different personas. We want to extend the life of our clothes if they are right for us. Staying faithful: recycling, reinventing.

The look is more natural. It is no longer about MAKE UP, it is all about MAKE DOWN, removing the plastic and artificial. It takes work to be this natural! We need an array of hair and make up products to achieve this simplicity. What we put on our skin we are essentially digesting into our bodies. The new generation of cosmetics uses organic ingredients that respect our skin and support our health. We want the products we use to be nutritional and chemical free.

good
enough
to eat

Jurlique, an Australian skin and body care company produces a range based on the principles of aromatherapy, ayurveda, homeopathy and alchemy. All the herbs and flowers are grown in a pollution-free environment without the use of chemical fertilizers, pesticides or insecticides, combining ancient methods of extraction with up-to-the-minute technology that preserves the regenerative 'life-force' properties of the plants. This gives the end product exceptional purity and potency. The company is Australia's fastest growing cosmetic company with year on year growth of between 50 and 100 per cent.

curiosity

question everything As children we have an insatiable curiosity. We are constantly asking questions. Somehow that spark dulls as we are educated into the 'way things are done'. Today, we are seeing a return of that innate curiosity. More of us are asking questions, wanting to learn about everyday things that we take for granted. Through learning, we come to appreciate that which we were previously unconscious of, giving our life an added depth of meaning. For instance, who was St Valentine and why do we celebrate his day? **Who** was Father Christmas?

Through technological advances we have less connection to the past. We want to know more about our history, to be reminded of our roots. We love to hear secrets of the past.

In 1998 the British Museum Press published *How To Read Egyptian Hieroglyphs* written by two British Egyptologists. This book offered the reader the chance to understand ancient inscriptions that had been otherwise incomprehensible to the curious tourist. The book sold 35,000 copies in the first six months.

We want to know all about the products we own. **WHERE** are they made? What is special about this specific one? For instance, when choosing tea, we want to know about the different kinds: specific details about the regions, their tastes and peculiarities. **WHAT** is first flush?

If a restaurant plays music, a music menu can give us details of the pieces and artists. WE WANT TO LEARN ON THE GO. Curiosity brings our attention to things we have not yet considered. But we don't have time to read books on specific topics. We want information brought to us in an easy way, popular versions of important scientific and sociological reports. Potted information that gives us the essence.

genderfusion

androgynous brain Men and women are equal yet different. The brain is divided into a 'masculine' left, analytical hemisphere and a 'feminine' right, intuitive hemisphere. Each of us has our own individual combination. If we go back several generations we can see the clear social differentiation between the sexes. How much of that behaviour was created by chemistry, and how much by social convention? Behaviour becomes chemistry, chemistry becomes behaviour.

role reversal

Socially, we are experiencing a breakdown of traditional stereotypes; for example, male nannies, women soldiers, men cooking, women buying and maintaining their own technical equipment, men deciding on colour, women doing extreme sports. With the rise of the women's movement there has been a push for equality. If it makes more sense for the father to stay at home and look after the children and the mother to be a primary wage earner, why not? We are seeing more and more unisex products. It is becoming acceptable to be androgynous. Combat trousers, khakis, fragrances, drinks, language. What is important is that we all feel free to experience life in our own individual way.

empowerment

This century has seen the awakening of women. Although institutionalized prejudice still exists, women have come together, struggled and discovered their strengths. Women today have more support and opportunity than ever before. However, men have been as much a victim of the patriarchal structure as women have. It might not be so obvious, but limitation goes both ways. More and more men are starting to question the limiting patriarchal model and are freeing themselves to discover something new.

Today we have the chance to develop that part of us that has been dormant for centuries, making us aware of the other aspects of ourselves. We no longer need to follow a rigid form.

birthdeath

from the womb to the tomb Life scares us. How many of us have been present at a birth or a death? The two major transitions in life, the two spiritual experiences that we are guaranteed. Once we enter life, one thing is certain: we are going to leave it. Although being born and dying appear to be two very different processes, at a certain level they are the same experience. The baby leaves the womb for the world, whilst the adult leaves the world for ... who knows?

Perhaps one of the reasons why our culture has tabooed these subjects is that they emphasize the uncertainty of our lives. Birth and death put us in touch with the real world. Life in its terrifying honesty, the beauty, power, joy and pain of being human. These experiences challenge our mind's comfortable beliefs and its ability to be in control. As a culture we are beginning to consciously participate in, acknowledge and honour these real-life processes.

birth

When a child is born it needs to feel welcomed, loved and wanted. Babies are conscious whilst they are in the womb. So the newly born will be shocked by forceps, bright lights, cold temperatures, chemicals and lack of human contact. Extensive reporting on these facts has made parents more aware. By expressing our preferences and making personal choices we are transforming the way we participate in the birth process.

Many of us feel safe with and require the conventional medical establishment, yet increasing numbers of people are choosing home births with support from midwives. Imagine hospitals with birth centres where the environment is specially designed to relax the mother and baby, supporting the birth process in a natural way with midwives, massage therapists, birthing pools and other alternatives. The support of our sophisticated, technological medicine would be available, but only when and if necessary.

Until that time, the alternative is a home birth. It is strange that such a development is seen as new. Women have been giving birth at home for thousands of years. We are rediscovering the power of birth, supporting each other and discovering our shared resources. It is equally important for fathers to play a role, supporting the mother and participating in the process. Birth is being reclaimed from the medical profession. We are finding a new model for birth as a rite of passage, ancient and yet modern, safe and empowering.

death

In many cultures death is integrated as part of life. But many of us do not know how to approach it or how to comfort those who lose loved ones. We are beginning to address this. Hospices and hospitals are training professionals to support the dying. We want our doctors and medical staff to approach their dying patients as humans and not hide behind professional detachment.

How do we want to die? It is time to transform our relationship with death. A few of us are choosing when to end our lives and leaving directives. This is transforming our view of euthanasia and the rigid beliefs that society has about dying. Deciding on the way we want to die enables us to die with dignity, a ***conscious death.*** For our loved ones this could be just the healing process necessary to help the family cope with the loss.

How would you like others to say goodbye? A DIY funeral can be denominational, cross-denominational or non-demominational: a scattering of ashes in a woodland; a quiet, meditative gathering or a riotous, drunken wake.

design
your
future

our work

work2000+

career creativity A company is an important social unit. It participates in the social process. The rise of project-based, temporary contracts means that more people are going to be moving from one job to another, with the responsibility for hiring out our skills resting firmly on our own shoulders. Due to the **portfolio** nature of the future job market this might be a responsibility that we have to get used to. How are we going to feel about this? State pensions will not provide sufficient income. Will we be working beyond retirement?

What is work really about? Is our working life time out from our real life? Do we work solely to be able to spend? Have we sacrificed creativity and meaning? Changes are taking place.

Both companies and individuals are searching for a new paradigm where ownership, initiative and creativity are part of the working partnership

integral restructuring

Many companies are questioning their structures. Do the hierarchical forms of the past still serve us? Do we need more integrated, democratic structures? A new framework gives a company the possibility to achieve new results. It can evolve towards being more innovative, productive, improving working relationships and increasing enjoyment. More enjoyment means less stress, better motivation and more efficiency.

new formats

In the future a large proportion of companies will be virtual. Some companies will have virtual departments, where a team of people will work together, possibly from different time zones. Each person can work according to their own needs and requirements and not be restricted by an office structure.

We will increasingly see teams created for particular projects for a specific time. Once the project is completed, the team is disbanded. This means an assignment can benefit from the best team from anywhere in the world. New managerial skills are required to manage this. It will mean balancing the needs of the company with the needs of each employee and involving them in forming and implementing policies.

other options are:

term-time working

employees remain on permanent contract as either full or part time, but have unpaid absence during school holidays.

hot desking

no individual desks or fixed telephones and computers. Employees book offices, workstations and meeting rooms when needed. An individual's regular workspace is a personal portable telephone and computer.

job sharing

two or more people share the responsibility of one full-time job, dividing pay, holidays and other benefits between them.

career breaks

an extended period of unpaid leave from work. The intention is that the employee will return to work with the same employer at the same job level.

annual hours

is a working system whereby the number of hours employees work is defined over the whole year and determined by the needs of the employee and the company.

flexi-time

allows employees to choose within set limits the times to start and finish. Also, carrying over hours allowing flexileave.

v-time

is voluntarily reduced work time schemes to allow to trade income for time off.

working from home

it is now possible to work at home while continuing to be part of a corporation, either full time, part time, freelance or e-lance, as a consultant or a researcher. By 2020, up to 25 percent of the workforce could be working from home.

New Ways to Work is a London-based charitable organization that advises on flexible working arrangements. Through research and education they aim to assist in the transformation of the workplace culture, to give freedom of choice to those who wish to work outside traditional patterns.

working life

We want our working lives to be human. A work environment of sexual and racial equality. Where the organization is committed to growing, to serving the stockholders, the employees and the public.

More companies are supporting the development of their workforce, learning about communication, conflict resolution, teambuilding and dealing with stress. There is a need for personal development and the learning of new skills. A conscious company can assist in this process. Our companies are going to need to become more socially engaged, giving work and support to the older generation.

support teams

In order for us to work we need support teams. Groups of helpers, domestics, shoppers, personal trainers. Larger companies have the capacity to provide services for their employees: child care, food, health centers, exercise places, to make life easier.

work space health space

The quality of the workplace has a huge influence on the quality of our work. Good air, light and sound nourish us, freeing creativity and increasing attention. The more uncomfortable and distracting the environment, the more difficult it is to work. By creating a space we enjoy working in, we develop a sense of belonging to the work space. Employers can add features such as kitchens, meditation rooms or exercise rooms. More companies are becoming interested in the concept of feng shui, energetic architecture and interior design. As these ideas are assimilated new office formats are developing.

British Airways have recently moved into an 'office of the future': open plan, virtually paperless, equipped with sofas and comfortable chairs, 'hot desks', 'quiet areas', supermarket, cafés, fitness centre, flower shop, hairdresser and a bank. Their 240 acres of reclaimed land creates a public park and nature reserve. The result has been considerable saving, less sickness, less hierarchy, shorter meetings, more flexibility, more energy, more informality, more work being done and a happier workforce.

work and technology

The development of technology means transformation of the way we work. We keep in touch via video conferencing, video phone and the internet. Companies are networking worldwide, creating intranet systems. These networks are designed to share information within a company. They are similar to the internet, but only accessible to the employees. The intranet will serve as the company headquarters.

Many of us will operate out of portable offices at home or on the go. This will create more time for human interaction.

corporate IQ

A corporation is like an organism. It needs to have full use of its resources. The more accessible these resources are, the greater the ability of the organism to act and react. Company databases are going to increase in size and ease of access. The increased capacity of digital processing allows companies the integrated awareness that goes beyond just a computer network. Systems will be able to synthesize, to take into account competitors, customers, accounts, future developments and past mistakes, and to creatively guide us in decision making, based on rich, accurate and immediate information.

the company's computer system will be as insightful as a senior board member

individuality

it's my life As consumers we are becoming more individual in our wants and preferences. We want to equip our lives according to our needs. We don't just want to buy something because it works, we want it to work for us, for our life. We don't want to be stereotyped, but treated as individuals who have unique lives. There is something meaningful in being able to participate in the creative process of product development. Companies are starting to understand this.

We want the retailer and manufacturer to understand that we have a life, we don't just fit into a pre-manufactured standard. 'Lifestyle' is dis-empowering: it is society's control over an individual's choice. We would like to choose the size, materials, colours, aromas and textures of the products we buy. What herbs would you like in your constitutional tonic? What essential oils would you like in your skin products? What colour would you like your computer? How big your bath? From cosmetics to home appliances,

we want to have our say

intimacy

We are experiencing a backlash against the technological society. We want more of a connection to the products we buy. When we go shopping we want the retailing environment to reflect these concerns. We don't want to be assaulted by abrasive sales assistants and impatient music trying to subliminally speed us to make the sale and get out! We want to feel at home, cared for, a sense of closeness and understanding. We want it to be an experience, a two-way communication between the products and ourselves.

caring consumer

sourcesmart We are attracted to companies that mirror our life concerns. As consumers we are increasingly helped in our search for ethical companies. There are consumer watch-dogs publishing details of companies' political and environmental activities and press articles informing our choices. We want to know if a company is supporting an oppressive regime, or using under-aged child labour to cut costs.

We want products that are non-harmful, with packaging that has been chosen with care and concern. We would like to know about a company. What is their history? Our conscience as consumers and human beings is one and the same. This dictates the choices that we make. We want companies to participate in this process. To clean up their acts and be honest with their information. We want

full product disclosures

so that our investments will be part of the planetary solution, not add to the problem. We are involved in creating the consumer culture of the future.

interaction

The consumer wants a relationship with the brand of their choice. What does that mean? As in any relationship, trust and loyalty form the basis of a lasting connection. Will bribing a consumer with special offers such as air miles and free gifts win their loyalty? It might for a while, but

a real bond is created through integrity, understanding and consideration

EasyJet, a budget airline, currently sells over one third of its travel tickets on-line through its web site. In November 1999 flight timetables became exclusively advertised on the web. The company's promise is to provide safe, low cost, good value air travel. In the event of delays over four hours the customer is sent a letter or fax, signed by the Chairman, apologizing for the inconvenience and refunding the cost of the ticket.

Itsu restaurant in London searches for intensity, flavour, and purity in the food it serves. A small booklet on each table states that Itsu is for people who value their time, their health and their quality of life. It is for people who are tired with formality and structure, wanting to replace this with convenience and freedom. The customers can choose dishes from a conveyer belt that moves around the restaurant counter. This does the work of 16 people. Savings are reinvested into quality ingredients. Itsu promises to put the customer in control.

The opinions and attitudes of the public change fast, we react to the information that is presented to us in the media. A leading brand could lose support overnight due to unfavourable media exposure that is poorly managed. It is in the best commercial interest of companies to maintain their integrity, and stay closer to the public.

product appeal

branding A brand is more than just a particular make of goods. It is the core of a **product family**. It reflects the characteristics and the personality of the whole. Once this has been established, we can create a family based on the same core qualities. These are communicated through labelling, wording, packaging, colour, graphics, advertising and public relations. It is expressed through the employees and the work-culture adopted.

what is the reason?

What makes this product different? So many products look the same. We are asking more questions: is it good for me? Will it make me happy? Will it make me feel safe, protected, in control of my life? Will it connect me, comfort me?
There needs to be a reason for a new product. The trend is towards streamlining and simplification of product lines. So if we introduce a new product, think about how it will stir the public's interest. Go for innovation, surprise, practicality, aesthetic value, different usage, time efficiency, quality, worth. Whatever we buy is on show somewhere in our lives, whether it is a washing up liquid or a shampoo.

we want to buy into brands that reflect our commitment to style, taste and integrity

From September 1999 Unilever will begin the process of reducing its portfolio of brands from the current 1,600 to a more slimmed-down concentration of 400 'power-brands'. The downsizing is intended to save a billion pounds a year in running costs, leading to a simpler, more effective supply chain, reducing complexity, increasing cost effectiveness and enhancing productivity.

concept and communication

The concept and communication behind the product is as important as the product itself. The labelling, language, packaging, colour and graphics all need to be considered at the start. How is the product going to sit at point of sale, and what is to be communicated? How is this going to be integrated into advertising and PR campaigns?

individual communication

As we become an information society, data gathering services will be collecting information on our habits. Which shops do we use our charge card in? Which web pages do we read? Through this intelligence gathering, a very precise consumer profile of us will be developed. This will lead to very specific targeting and different advertising for different consumers. By knowing the consumer's interests and what they buy, a company can interact with them, offering products and services for their personal lives. Whilst lifestyle marketing is aimed at a certain way of living, we are now marketing to our customers' life, not style.

holistic communication

The communication of a brand has to reflect its attributes. No false stories, no more false promises. Layering the message consistently, attribute by attribute. CREATING A MULTI LEVEL SANDWICH OF THE PRODUCT'S PERSONALITY and communicating this through different media: print advertising, public relations, endorsement of real-life models. Educating and at the same time entertaining. Bringing the product alive with a story, a sense of understanding, compassion and desirability.

shopping

consumer choice On-line shopping is increasing in popularity. It is quick and easy. What will we purchase on-line? Most goods and services: books, videos, cds, cars, travel (flights, car hire, hotels, holidays), clothing, stocks and shares, food and flowers. On-line window shopping gives an opportunity to visit innumerable shops from home, comparing and researching different options.

Nike recently opened its largest store in the world in London. Nike Town provides customers with an interactive leisure world by creating a multimedia sporting experience in the store. Information on where specific sports can be played locally, sports clinics, visits from sports celebrities and information displays create a leisure experience.

the experience

If we can purchase the majority of what we need through the net why do we need to go shopping? We will expect something more. We want an experience. Shopping becomes an activity of learning, enjoyment and entertainment. Retailers will study the exact profile of their customers and project their messages through the interactive communication of multimedia imagery. Responsive displays can change according to the aspirations and interests of customers. As a consequence retailers will be able to give a personalized service as well as offering products that customers actually want.

Stores will reflect their brand image through multi-functional environments where customers can experience the brand's image as well as its products. The shopping experience will bring brands alive.

old style

The market is where it all began. Markets are community institutions that support our area. They are full of life, colour, people and energy. A place where we can get fresh local produce: flowers, eggs, vegetables, herbs, bread, fish and meat. Often we will find local variations of fruit and vegetables not available in the supermarket. Currently some supermarkets are experimenting with giving space to local farmers and allowing them to sell their produce.

In 1997 the first farmers' market opened in Bath. Currently more than 55 towns in the UK have farmers' markets. Local farmers sell their fruit, vegetables, juice, cheese, herbs, meat, wine, eggs and bread directly to the public, giving the public the chance to buy a greater variety of fresh produce, talk to the farmers and support small family farms.

bulking

There are many products we use daily and need to replace weekly. Bulk buying saves on packaging and time. Instead of buying box after box of cornflakes we can scoop them out of huge cereal bins into the recycled bag we have brought with us. We want our supermarkets to take the initiative, to actively participate in reducing waste and offer an extensive range of bulk goods: nuts, dried fruits, cereals, grains, pastas, honey, maple syrup, oils, flours, chocolates, cleaning materials and so on.

mail order

Catalogues will continue to be a choice as we can explore our options comfortably at home. Most mail order companies have on-line facilities, enabling them to achieve a faster service. We will see an increase in specialist product catalogues, such as beauty, gardening and books.

bargains

Charity shops, flea markets and car boot sales offer opportunities to find bargains and quality goods. Although it is not for all, those with imagination and time can be rewarded with unexpected treasures.

money

cashless society The financial sector is also affected by change. Our technology is developing new ways for the financial system to operate. We are moving towards a cashless society. Using debit cards (to replace cheques), credit cards, smart cards and e-cash. The e-wallet will replace cash altogether. Cash will be a thing of the past. There are dangers to these developments. We will no longer be in touch with the unit of exchange. It becomes an abstraction, something that exists on paper, in a computer chip.

electronic cash

E-cash will be a substitute for cash. It is stored in an embedded chip placed on an electronic debit card. It offers many benefits: convenience, speed and flexibility.

electronic wallet

Smart card technology will allow cards to function as electronic wallets. Smart cards are similar to e-cash, yet their embedded chips have the ability to track and store information on consumer spending and other data. These cards will be more secure than e-cash as access will be guarded through sophisticated identification codes. Civil liberty groups are concerned that the smart-card will limit our freedom as it could allow governments and institutions to gather information on us. These technological developments are supposed to increase our freedom, not take it away.

cyber finance

As an industry, banking is wired to the latest technological developments. The internet has invented e-cash. It opens up a whole new financial world and theoretically gives anybody the opportunity to establish a private currency. The internet also allows us to become our own fund managers. On-line activities include investment, brokerage services and the ability to chat to fellow investors and experts. We are able to research corporate web sites and other worldwide investment opportunities.

green banking

More of us are concerned where we bank. Once we put our hard-earned money into our bank we lose control of it. We don't want to support a bank that invests irresponsibly. Banks, like other businesses, need to be in agreement with the values of their customers – expressing a commitment to the environment, a respect for human rights and a concern for the welfare of the community.

In 1992, the Co-operative Bank announced its spearheading ethical policy. The company refuses to invest in, or provide financial services to, those businesses it considers abuse the environment, oppress the human spirit or are involved in the cruel treatment of animals. The bank released dual mission statements, one guaranteeing to its customers a continuing high-quality service and the other pledging to the community to uphold its ethical principles. It is their belief that a clear conscience is the strongest foundation on which to build a successful business.

local currency

We are becoming more creative with money. Local exchange trading systems (lets) and community currencies are being introduced. These methods of exchange promote community resilience and sustainability, ensuring that money remains in the local economy. A lets scheme is a mini economy. The different members list their services and commodities. They then trade with other community members, exchanging skills and goods. Within this scheme people are able to buy and sell much like the main economies. Such systems are currently operating in the UK and US.

global currency

In recent years economics has been a catalyst for increased unification between countries. In 2002 Europe will be united under a common currency. Perhaps this is the beginning of a larger movement towards a global currency? If the Euro works, many people will begin to think about the possible advantages of working with a single global economy.

english language

english – the global language English is becoming the global language. If something is written or translated into English it becomes accessible to the whole world. The worlds of business, science, computers, marketing, design and air and sea travel all use English for communication.

How is English evolving? As our society develops, so does the language and its grammar. We are constantly making new words. Two important developments that are influencing our language and communication are the vocabularies from biology and cyber space.

bio language

Physics has been a dominant science in our culture, influencing our perception and language. As environmental issues and biological engineering become mainstream, the influence of biological language is becoming evident. Words convey an understanding outside of their original field of meaning. **PRODUCT DNA** refers to a product's make-up and characteristics. Other words include 'cell structures', 'replication', 'mutation', 'organicity'.

cyber language

The internet and e-mail are new ways in which we communicate with each other. Cyber language is developing its own symbols giving personality to communication on line: a happy face, a tear, hurt feelings and abbreviations such as U2, lol, IM etc. Through the growth of cyberspace we will see the infiltration of other languages into our own.

Watch out as our language becomes **WORD–BYTES.** Soon we will be using these words in our everyday language.

Though the world's people speak approximately 6,000 languages, it is estimated that English is now spoken by more than one fifth of the world's population. There is an increase in the number of new spoken Englishes. Singaporeans, for example, can speak Singlish, which is a combination of three languages and is unintelligible to the foreigner.

awareness

consciousness as a commodity The quality of our thinking is reflected in the quality of our work. Our sensitivity and awareness are our assets. The depth of our clarity, stability and insight depends on the state of our mind. These attributes have to be cultivated, they have to be worked at and don't just happen on their own. Solitude, spending time with nature, removing psychological obstacles and meditating all help to cultivate consciousness. Discovering which tools work for us and applying these accordingly will bring greater enjoyment, ease, productivity and empowerment to our lives.

imagineering

Imagineering is the engineering of imagination and intelligence. By using our left-brain intelligence and our right-brain imagination we can use our mental capabilities to **THE FULLEST. THE MORE WE CAN MOVE BEYOND OUR LIMITED HABITUAL WAYS OF THINKING AND RELATING TO THE WORLD, THE MORE WE ARE ABLE TO BE CREATIVE.** Discovering new possibilities that we were not able to access previously.

We need to step outside the old, limiting mindset and come up with new ways of approaching problems. **OUR SUCCESS WILL COME FROM EXPLORING AND CHALLENGING OURSELVES AND THE WAY THINGS HAVE BEEN DONE.** The market is not static, there is constant change. So we need to change with it, to update and stay fresh. The ability to think creatively leads to new products and services as well as financial rewards.

imagination,intuition
and intelligence
are the hottest properties

Shell's recent senior international management meeting in Maastricht, the Netherlands, was part of the company's strategic transformation programme, changing their structure and the way people relate to each other. Guest speakers presented Shell management with a variety of differing mindsets and perspectives that challenged the participants to think differently and more openly about the future. Lama Yeshe Losal, the abbot of Samye Ling Tibetan Monastery, was one of the guest speakers. He talked about the importance of respecting and caring for the world and gave a meditation instruction recommending the value of meditation as a way of dealing with the stress of today's business.

James H. Austin, MD, Professor Emeritus of Neurology at the University of Colorado Health Sciences Center has recently authored *Zen and the Brain* (MIT Press). The book integrates the mystical and the scientific in an exploration of the physiological and chemical brain changes brought about by Zen Buddhist practice.

design
your
future

our society

art transforms

artist as messenger What purpose does art serve in our lives and in our culture? Art is the expression of the creative psyche, artists explore the dreams of humanity, expressing the vital spirit of life. It shakes us, shocks us, wakes us up, helping us to confront those things that we would rather not look at. Art is not just for adorning our homes, collecting, or hanging in galleries. **Art is communication with the human essence.**

Art is good for your health! Through enjoying art, whether exploring our own creativity or appreciating another's, we transform. Our mood lifts, we receive fresh inspiration, and even our brain chemistry can change. Artists bring the messages that our culture needs to listen to and learn. Each of us can discover our own artistic side. But living in a world of 'art critics' it is challenging for us to go beyond our perfectionist judgements of ourselves.

synthesis of forms

The increasing sophistication of our technology is altering our assumptions about what art is. Computers and virtual reality open a whole new universe of experimentation and creativity. Download art off the Net: virtual galleries, symphonic creations, murals, graffiti, poetry and photography all exist in digital imagery. Artists are embracing this melting pot of synthesis and experimentation, mixing forms: classical, soul, funk, house and poetic rap. Interactive art is encouraging us to participate, to be inside the installation or drama. As our planet becomes more interconnected we are exposed to our rich planetary traditions of music, dance, writing and painting. We are as interested in archaic Aboriginal music and Tibetan sand mandalas as we are in Bach and Warhol.

fringe becomes mainstream

Public Enemy, Ice T and the Beastie Boys are amongst the growing number of music artists who have released their work directly onto the Net. It has been estimated that a total of 17 million tracks are downloaded each day.

At the recent Bienale Exhibition in Venice, Tatsuo Miyajima presented the 'Revive Time' Kaki Tree Project. The seedlings from a Kaki tree that survived the atomic destruction of Nagasaki have become the symbols for a project that supports the development of world peace, connecting the energy of life across the globe through the adoption of the seedlings. The 'Revive Time' project is constantly changing, integrating interactive events, art exhibitions, planting ceremonies, a web site and a publication.

new tradition

contemporary rituals Traditions are important for us. They give us cultural attachment, connecting us to our communities, the past and our ancestors. Our customs are disappearing under the influence of our consumer culture. The Christian tradition no longer has the influence that it used to. The Christian year with its festivals and celebrations is slowly dissolving. We are now living in a multi-religious society in which many different traditions are represented.

All that remains of what was once our sacred calendar are the celebrations from which retailers make a profit. We are suffering from a lack of authentic celebrations.

we want to find new ways to celebrate local and global traditions of remembrance

If we are to infuse our lives with meaning we need to question our holidays.

Why do we have a Christmas tree? Is there a relationship between the evergreen pine and the birth of Jesus Christ? Is it because the tree is an ancient symbol? Does the tree represent the principle of life at the darkest time of the year, the winter solstice? We need to understand the history and meaning of our rituals.

we want festivals that reflect the concerns of today's world

Festivals and holidays in which we can all participate, irrespective of our religious philosophy. A common ground on which we can all relate, perhaps based on the seasonal cycles. How about events to celebrate the aspirations of our global community? Hiroshima Peace Day, Jubilee 2000, Earth Day. Global integration is inevitable. We can begin to celebrate the life that we have in common.

On April 22 1970, 20 million Americans celebrated the first Earth Day, a grass roots national holiday in support of nationwide environmental education. It has continued every year as a local community and school celebration, becoming a worldwide event in support of the preservation of our planet for future generations.

livingwith nature

planet earth Our culture is experiencing a change in its relationship with the natural world. We are acknowledging our interdependence. We know that unless we take on environmental responsibility and stewardship, our children are not going to have clean air and water. The sun will kill instead of give life. Ecosystems will break down and life will be threatened with extinction.

Like our own immune system, the immune system of our planet is being compromised by stress. This is dangerous and threatening for the whole planetary ecology.

environmental thinking

There is a basic sanity to ecological thinking. Far from being idealistic, it is the most realistic way to build a culture that will last and support all of us.

Children are the new generation of environmentalists. They are interested in protecting and learning about the world in which we live. We are the guardians of the planet for future generations. We are all becoming concerned by changing weather patterns, global warming, increased chemical, nuclear and biological pollution. It makes us think. We need more **COLLECTIVE RESPONSIBILITY AND ACTION** to protect and restore the environment for ourselves and our future. We need long-term thinking. The public imagination is ready for a shift. We are tired of viewing the future as a negative, post-nuclear, technocratic nightmare. We want a change of scenario. We are seeing more people develop **ECO–OPTIMISM,** acknowledging that we can do something. We can participate in making a collective shift. It all starts at home.

living with nature

We will have to build a friendship between nature and our culture. Looking towards how we can support the environment and not exploit it.

We can bring this change into our daily lives by participating in recycling schemes and supporting environmental organizations and conservation initiatives. Thoughtful consumption of paper, water and energy helps reduce waste. We can rediscover the earth and support that process by bringing the natural world more into our lives. Enjoying the plant kingdom by filling our houses and gardens, streets and shopping centres with vegetation and trees. We will gain immense pleasure from living closer to the natural world.

youngage oldage

young at heart What is age? Is it chronological, measured by the passing of time? Is it biological, measured by the body? Or is it attitudinal, measured by our experience of life? These are the questions that we will all ask ourselves as we get older. Research will provide us with a new science of rejuvenation. But we cannot put all the responsibility on modern medicine. We have a **choice** as to how we experience our later years. We will become **conscious agers** as we question assumptions regarding ageing.

Our environment, food, emotions and mental attitudes eventually become our biology. If we believe we should retire at 60 and start preparing for death at 75, who knows the influence that idea has on our biology? A long, satisfying life means a healthy life: living in a healthy environment, positive mental attitude, emotional expression, enjoyable work, close intimate relationships, a balanced diet, some exercise, learning and working to stay mentally alert.

elders

In recent years the older generation has been excluded from participating in the family and community. This is partly due to our society's worship of youth and partly due to the resistance of older generations towards change. In order to have a valuable role, elders need to be more flexible and understanding, being able to give the wisdom of their experience and relate it to the needs of the time. If we have no elders of our own we will adopt them.

Since we have a culture that centres around the activities of the young, we are less interested in those no longer participating in that world. However, as our seniors become healthier and younger in attitude they want an active role. What will be the contribution of those elders to the needs of our society ?

Age is becoming interchangeable between the generations. We all wear the same clothes, read the same, eat the same, and are even beginning to speak the same language! New dialogues are developing.

Looking at the ancient and indigenous cultures as a guide, we see that the elders served an important function in maintaining the framework of society. They fulfilled the role of spiritual guides, family leaders and mentors.

there is
no substitute
for the wisdom
of experience

protection

do not disturb In our society, peace, quiet and privacy have become luxuries we need to work to attain. Our privacy is encroached upon. We are challenged by undesirable light, smells and sounds. We have to deal with junk mail, 'spam' (internet junk mail) and telephone soliciting. We are going to find new ways of protecting our privacy. Personal consultants specializing in privacy and security are going to help us guard our sanctuary from the busy world.

Some of us are choosing to live in gated communities. But most choose to rely upon modern technology, installing the latest alarm systems, automatic lighting, electric fencing and other security measures. But we also need to feel secure within ourselves. Otherwise, with all these measures, we will only seal ourselves off from the rest of the world, making us even more fearful and isolated.

foodrink

eat to live Organic makes sense. It is wholesome. Our brain, heart, nerves and other organs are affected by the food we eat. When we eat organic food our body does not have to process chemicals, giving itself the chance to regenerate and strengthen. **We become what we eat**. Our diet is all important.

A diet heavy in processed foods affects our whole system: skin, nervous system, digestion and immune system. It puts our whole body out of balance, interfering with our internal communication, making us less sensitive to what we need. Processed food has little fibre to make the digestion work, so it's harder to recognize when we have eaten enough.

The organic choice is a consumer choice. As more people buy organic, the price will go down. The agribusiness supports a limited variety of produce. Traditionally, there were many regional crop variations. As community-supported agriculture develops and market gardening increases, we are seeing a re-emergence of the traditional varieties of produce that we had lost. It is not necessary to eat food grown on the other side of the world. By supporting local produce we begin to eat in cycle with the seasons, which is what our bodies were designed for.

Since our bodies are 70 percent water, it is essential that the water we drink is of a good quality. Mineral waters, flavoured waters, purified waters. Start looking for water with added vitamins, herbs, oxygen and natural flavours.

H_2O, it's the drink

organic poisons

We like our indulgences and we want those to be organic as well. We will see the growth of organic spirits and tobacco as well as chocolate and wines.

organic cool

Organic produce and restaurants have traditionally had a wholesome, homey feel. This is changing. Packaging is treated with the same design standard as other foods, using leading designers. Store and restaurant design is becoming sophisticated and modern. The new places to go to.

fast healthfood chains

Sales of organic food in the UK are likely to triple in the next four years. Last year the increase was 40 percent. Planet Organic, the largest organic supermarket in London, has seen increases of 35 percent year on year since it opened in 1995. Two more sites are planned to open this year to ultimately form a chain of 30. Planet Organic's customers are mainly professionals. This year they will develop a line of fresh fast organic food to take away.

nutriceuticals

At the other end of the spectrum to organic food we are seeing the development of super-foods. Foods that no longer look like foods, but are bars, gels, pills and powders technically designed for broad spectrum nutrition, supplementing and substituting normal food. With specialist knowledge we are also designing food for the brain, for energy, relaxation, immunity and other functions. **SUPERFOODS** that not only feed us, but also help to support our optimal functioning.

your constitution

We all come in different colours, shapes and sizes. We are individuals with preferences and predispositions for certain emotions and ways of thinking. Our bodies are also very different: each of us has an individual bio-energetic, chemical, genetic and hormonal make up. The ways that our bodies work are similar, yet individual. Our bodies need different fuel. We can eat ourselves into balance by giving ourselves what we need. Some of us need to eat more, others need less, for some raw food corrects an imbalance, whilst for others it would weaken them. As we take more of an interest in what we need, we find that it becomes very individual. There really are no rules, only guidelines. As we learn to trust ourselves more and nutritional science embraces constitutional differences, we will be able to find the diet that works perfectly for our body.

eat
yourself
well

integral medicine

holism Holism is the treatment of the whole person rather than just the disease. Holistic medicine has been practised for thousands of years. Today we are witnessing a resurgence of interest in these traditions: Chinese medicine, acupuncture, ayurveda and homeopathy. **These medicines address the energetic imbalances that can cause physical diseases.**

In these traditional systems of healing, disease is often seen to be caused by disharmony between the mind, the emotions and the soul. Modern medicine is exploring these conclusions.

Bodywork techniques such as Alexander technique, Feldenkreis, aromatherapy and massage help to support better psychological and physical health, releasing somatic and energetic blocks so that the body functions properly.

In treating a life-threatening case, the allopathic physician can make choices for surgical measures, chemotherapy, pharmaceuticals or other treatments. But after the danger has passed, alternative treatments can assist the patient in re-balancing the system so that the body can heal.

Exeter University's Centre for Complementary Health Studies reports that there are 40,000 complementary therapists in the UK compared to 36,000 family doctors. They see in excess of three million clients each year.

allopathic medicine (orthodox western medicine)

The newest development in Life Science is the mapping of human genes. Pharmaceutical giants and leading laboratories are pooling information to design a new picture of humanity. They plan to identify the tiny differences in our genetic code that indicate a tendency for specific diseases, such as asthma, diabetes and Alzheimer's disease. This knowledge could lead to medical treatments tailored specifically to individuals: which diseases might we be prone to? Which drug will we respond to best? This development paves the way for an entirely new kind of medicine.

the health of the nation

By integrating conventional and complementary treatment we have an opportunity to prevent a considerable amount of disease. Preventative education makes sense and cuts the costs of extensive medical care later on in life. We should invest in programmes of education and prevention, establishing healthy living centres that incorporate all aspects of health, diet and psychology. If state medical care provided preventative education and therapies we would all enjoy a better standard of health.

The Integrated Medical Centre is a pioneering new clinic in London, which takes the best of ancient and modern medicine and integrates them under one roof. The IMC is run by 21 qualified doctors and practitioners, each of whom is a leading specialist in their field, be it complementary or traditional medicine. The IMC approach is to treat the person, not the disease. By dealing with the issues around our emotional health, physical being and lifestyle they create an individualized programme to help the body heal itself.

technology

scientific responsibility Man can travel to the other side of the planet in a day, talk on a hands-free mobile phone whilst walking down the street, genetically alter plants and animals and even replace hearts with artificial organs. Although technology has definitely made certain tasks easier to perform, has it actually made our lives any easier? With every device we develop to save time we seem to be that much busier. First we develop a technology, and then it develops us! We cannot stop technological development, but we can acknowledge that we need to educate ourselves and be concerned about ethical considerations and long term effects.

For instance, although atomic energy provides us with efficient power, it has also left us with waste that will be dangerously radioactive for thousands of years. We will be long-buried when our children and their progeny have to deal with the poisonous refuse. As OUTER TECHNOLOGY develops we need to develop an INNER TECHNOLOGY, cultivating the awareness needed to work with these powerful new tools in a responsible manner. We need to be ready.

information

We are all aware that we are living in the information age. There is more information available now than in the accumulation of world history. The speed at which we can process is getting faster and faster. The planet is going on-line.

virtual reality

Virtual technologies will give us access to information not just through a screen, but directly into our senses through the use of helmets, goggles and hi-tech contact lenses. We are going to be able to explore cyber space, visit multimedia libraries or even go to school in a foreign country. We will be able to interact with other world inhabitants, visit our doctor, lawyer or accountant. A whole new world will open up for discovery.

machine talk

We want things to be easier! We want to have simple human–machine voice recognition, so that we can talk to our devices and operate them verbally. 'Lights on, lights off.' 'What is the quickest way to the airport today?' 'Turn the oven on to 330 degrees at a quarter past seven. Cook for an hour.' We want the keyboard to become obsolete!

At M.I.T. in Boston, the Affective Computing Research Group is working to create computers with the ability to recognize and respond to human emotions. The research into 'human-centred computers' aims to make fundamental improvements in the ability of the computer to serve us, reducing human-computer frustration.

clean power

One of the big scientific quests of our generation will be to discover a cheap and sustainable source of energy. There is a possibility that fossil fuels will run out in the next century, so we need to find non-polluting alternatives. It is time we found a quieter, cleaner option for cars. Imagine the cities without their pollution, perhaps just a quiet hum coming from electrical engines. It would have a huge impact on the quality of urban life.

As an alternative to fossil-fuelled cars, MotorDevelopment International, a French company, has built a zero pollution car (ZP) that runs on air! Cold pressurized air is pumped into a 770cc engine that contains hot air. The resulting reaction creates enough energy to power the vehicle. The car can run for ten hours and has a maximum speed of 55 mph. The car has the advantage of a carbon filtering system that allows it to suck in polluted urban air and blow out purified air. Dina, a Mexican government licensee, is contracted to produce an estimated 40,000 ZP taxis and urban delivery vehicles each year.

nanotechnology

We are going to be developing machinery smaller than living cells. By using an atom stacking mechanism, we can build micro-machinery from atoms. Tiny devices so small that they could travel through capillaries and repair damaged cells. At that level of magnification, machine and human can synthesize in undreamed-of ways. Our machines could be constructed down to the size of a blood cell, able to work faster than anything we can now imagine. These systems could be assembled into intelligent machines that contain trillions of such nanoscopic processing units.

psychotechnology

We are going to see the development of machines that can be used to develop the untapped potential of the human brain and mind. Helping us to balance left and right brains, access different states of mind and gain control over physical functioning that we believed to be involuntary. What once might have taken years to actualize, we will be able to achieve at the flick of a switch. Technology helps us to unleash the capacities of the brain that in turn will lead to the development of further possibilities.

There is no escape from the influence of technology. We cannot opt out. It is curious that those who have made the best attempts in the past to predict where technology might take us have been science fiction writers.

We are stepping into a science fiction future...

• High definition television • Video-on-demand • Palmtop computers • Public internet kiosks • Robotic surgeons • Artificial intelligence • Cloning • Voice and finger print recognition and activation • Automated habitat systems: computer-controlled households (air, light, water, heat) • Smart clothing: clothing with sewn-in communication and computer features • Micro-chip implants: storing personal information in our bodies • Genetic libraries: data storage facilities for plant, animal, and human DNA • Chi kung machines: technology to 'charge' us up with bio-energy • Bio-electric limb regeneration: stimulating bio-energy field to re-grow limbs • Cryobiology: science of preserving bio-matter through low temperatures • Human interface: direct human-machine communication • Bio-computers: computers made from organic materials (cells, nerves, etc.) • Nuclear fusion: source of clean nuclear energy • Tesla technology: electro-propulsion, zero point 'free' energy, and alternative physics pioneered by Nikola Tesla and other researchers • Ion propulsion: drive system for long-distance space travel • Virtual Retinal Display: visual input from computers direct into the eye.

habitats

our haven Our homes are places of retreat from the outside world, allowing us the time and space to recharge, reflecting our needs, concerns and individuality. In the past interior design was about creative ways to fill space. We are now seeing greater emphasis placed on the essential, uncluttering our living space so that we can enjoy the fundamental qualities of space and light. By paying more attention to space, we paradoxically emphasize the objects within it. Every object we own is harmoniously positioned so that its aesthetics, history and purpose are communicated.

We will see larger living spaces connecting to kitchens, eating areas, secluded bedrooms and bathrooms. Custom-built rooms for specifics such as yoga, carpentry and laundry. Feng Shui and energetic design applied to everything, even the garden. Gardens to be used as outdoor rooms, plants and flowers bringing nature closer to home.

multi-functional space

Increasingly, a large number of our activities are taking place at home, blurring the boundaries between work and home. This means we will be working, learning, entertaining, exercising, relaxing and schooling all in the same space. We need a workable space for all this. Probably larger homes for families.

Urban Splash, in the North West of the United Kingdom, is a new generation development company dedicated to the transformation of the urban environment. They are creating quality living, working and playing environments that are user-friendly, energy-efficient and reflect the new spirit of community. At present the current and completed schemes have provided 600 homes, 2,500 jobs and investment close to £100 million to tired areas of Liverpool and Manchester.

maintenance

We will design our homes so that they are easy to maintain and practical. Light, sound, security, air quality and cleaning can be automated. We are rediscovering the cleaning methods of the past, using old fashioned materials: vinegar, beeswax, soda, linseed oil; creating delicious smells of the past. We will take care in looking after things, being faithful to our belongings. Cleaning and maintenance will be tasks for all to share.

The German firm Seimens has developed a Home Electronic System. With the flick of a single switch the alarm system can be set, the temperature controlled, the lights and electrical appliances turned off. Phillips has developed a handheld system that controls home entertainment and regulates atmospheric conditions like lighting and temperature.

flexi-homes

Our homes will adapt to our lives. Simple design will allow us to easily change the function and mood. Flexible walls, electrical installations, furniture with 'add ons' and lighting will make it possible for us to transform our living space as our life and needs change. Perhaps we adapt our home to the seasons: a more extroverted lay-out in the summer or a den-feel for the winter months.

traditional techno

Quality counts. We will invest in well-made, traditional products: tables, chairs, beds. Archetypal shapes with additions: armchairs with swivel top tables, sofas with entertainment controls. As we mix the old with the new, technology with comfort, we are creating new functions.

by hand

Earthenware, wrought iron, glass, wood, matted grasses: these real goods speak their own language. There is greater value in an object with a story. It has spent days, perhaps weeks, under the hand of another person, whose energy and dreams are infused into the work. These objects bring the power of meaning into our homes, connecting us to a larger story.

greenbuilding

Buildings that are better for the environment are better for people. Green building incorporates environmentally responsible technology and materials, energy efficiency, good indoor air quality, resource conservation and ecological construction and maintenance. More of us will design, build and remodel on these principles, creating sustainable and environmentally responsible architecture.

one stop eco building merchants

London's largest and oldest housing association, the Peabody Trust, is investing ten million pounds in a project with the Bio-Regional Development Trust to develop 100 energy-efficient houses. The Zero Energy Development housing in Sutton will be the best example of urban sustainable living in the UK. The project includes the generation of energy entirely from renewable sources, a total water saving strategy, tele-working and office facilities, a sports club, nursery, organic shop and health centre.

Conde Nast, the producer of the world's most sophisticated magazines, including *Vogue*, the *New Yorker* and *Vanity Fair* have recently moved in to the world's first recycled skyscraper in New York. It is the leading project of its size to adopt ecological standards through energy efficiency and the use of sustainable materials and indoor ecology. The company supports the principles of responsible construction, operations and maintenance procedures.

social migration

urban possibilities We want our cities to become better places to live. We are looking at an urban regeneration. Cities have enormous potential as places of culture, work and entertainment. There will be a community approach to city planning. Mixing concentrated living areas with shops, bars, restaurants and pedestrian areas with parks, shared gardens and agricultural space, we can create a community experience. We are increasingly seeing inner city areas being regenerated.

Green development will integrate ecology and construction. Consideration will be given to families with children, with community areas and recreation centres. Towns will become quieter and more breathable places.

rural

The demands of rural life are very different to the demands of city living. The developments in communication technology mean that we have more of an opportunity to live outside cities, enjoy the benefits of the country and yet stay connected to the office. Younger people are moving to the country, bringing back multigenerational life

back to the village

Many of us will live in the country, working from home and spending a few days a week doing business in town or abroad.

moving to another country

As companies go global there will be a massive increase in people going to live and work abroad. Cheaper communication, travel and a common language will help us adapt to changing circumstances. The experience will offer us the opportunity to appreciate other cultures.

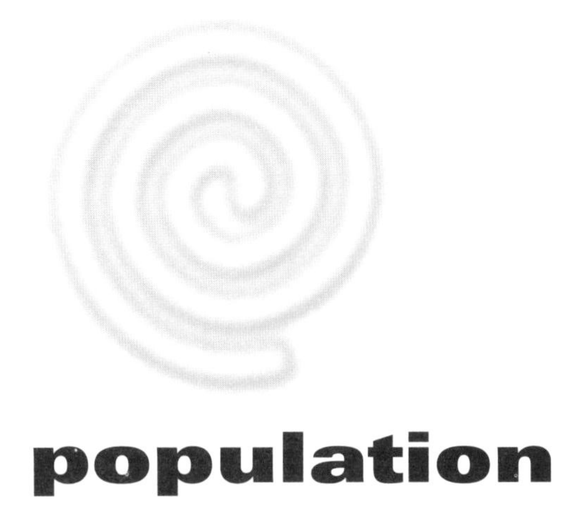

population

family size In the past we needed large families. It was a matter of survival, as it was likely that some of our children would die in infancy. The survivors were needed to work and look after the older generation. We now have a whole different set of concerns. Do we have enough raw materials and space to accommodate large families, while ensuring quality of life? A large family becomes an economic liability, employment is uncertain for the children, and parents need to commit to many years of financial support.

We are asking questions around the role of the family. If having children is no longer a question of survival, then what reasons do we have for building a family? We have the choice as to whether we want a family. More of us are choosing a smaller family so we are able to give more energy and time to our children.

In the commercially underdeveloped world, large families are still the traditional way of ensuring economic security. There is no other option. It is our responsibility to provide economic and educational support to release these nations from the burden of poverty and debt.

parenting

starts here We are the product of thousands of years of reproduction. Many of us assume that we will get married and have children, but do we actually question why we raise a family? The family is the basic social unit of society and therefore the quality of parenting is a reflection of the quality of our society. We need to examine our parenting and question how we raise our children, making changes so that our children do not inherit the issues and problems that their parents have ignored.

We need to offer future parents opportunities to learn about parenting, to be given theoretical and practical experience in parenting skills, communication, nutrition and basic healthcare. An open school for those who want to learn. We are no longer so close to the natural world that we can rely on our instincts!

With a 20-year track record in support of the family, Positive Parenting aims to provide information, training and resources to equip parents and those who assist them. Their materials are being used in a wide variety of circumstances, such as parent and toddler groups, schools and neighbourhood support centres.

We are acknowledging that parenting is a choice. We no longer assume that everybody wants to be a parent. Parenting is a life-long discipline of patience, sacrifice and love. A very natural way for us to serve humanity. But unless it is a conscious choice, parenting can overwhelm and limit both the parents and the children. More of us are choosing not be parents, to be creative without procreation, to offer and serve through other means.

In current society raising a family is the concern of only two people, who need to have both the time and the income to afford children. There is wisdom in the extended family that we have lost. The nuclear family is a stressed social unit. In many traditional cultures it is acknowledged that it takes a whole community to support the development of a child. Today many of us rely on two people, hired help and a television screen. We need to find new ways of raising a family, ways that allow us to enjoy the experience and have enough time for ourselves. Will we again be interested in communal living? Forming parental co-operatives to support each other?

school
for
parents

education

for life Education has a major influence upon our collective future. We need education that prepares us for life. What do our children need that will equip them to make the most of their lives? Is it more advice on health, drugs, sex, relationships and social skills, money, parenting, caring for the environment or careers?

Our educational systems are changing. An important part of this is the acknowledgement of

age appropriate learning

The discovery that the brain best learns certain functions at specific ages. If we introduce particular skills too early it confuses the mind.

Intelligence is not a matter of a high IQ. It comes in many forms: auditory, visual, spatial, emotional, musical, linguistic and kinesthetic. These skills are just as important as logic and memory. Each of us has a blend of these and learns with a different approach: storytelling, logical, philosophical, experimental. How do we build a system that supports us all?

educational establishments

We need to look at transforming educational institutions. We want to see schools built on the principles of community: less hierarchy, more trust, distributed responsibility, and effective communication.

A school need no longer look like a school. Instead of relying on blocks of resources it could operate as a core of overlapping networks. Learners would have an opportunity to use any of the resources available through the network. This system would be based on organic principles. Less mechanical, less regulated, less predictable and more creative. Obviously young children need a sense of family, of stability, within the classroom. But for older pupils and mature learners this could be an inventive educational experience.

We want to be part of a system where the role of the authorities is to stimulate and sustain excellence and creativity from within. Perhaps this is a matter of **DE-SCHOOLING SCHOOLS** and opening them up to become neighbourhood learning centres. The school need no longer be designed for a specific age, but instead address the learning needs of all ages, offering a range of services, combining education with social, cultural and financial information and resources.

the learner

The focus needs to move from the needs of the learning establishment to the needs of the learner. As learners we want a more active learning partnership. We want to individualize our studies and to participate in their planning, organization and assessment. Theory should be married to active learning projects where the students get experience in specific fields. Voluntary organizations, neighbourhood projects, manufacturers, offices, media and other organizations should be involved in the education system. In this way we begin to weave a culture of learning and appreciation. Together we can participate in our society's education.

The experiences of outward bound expeditions, team exercises and vocational courses broaden the experience and ability of the student. During our education our strengths and weaknesses need to be recognized and addressed in a creative way.

assessment

Traditionally our level of achievement has been assessed through the examination process. Yet according to multiple intelligence, theory examinations are to the advantage of only certain qualities of intelligence. Exams mostly reflect the memorization of formal knowledge.

We want to be able to give a balanced and fair assessment of pupils' abilities. To do that we can introduce other processes to complement exams, such as projects, videos, debates, presentations and a portfolio and assessment based on the learners' educational process. We need to find ways to help all of us succeed. We all have the capacity to live a creative, successful life. We just need support in unfolding what our inherent gift to the world is. This is the mission of the future educational system.

The new British National Curriculum has shifted in emphasis from the traditional to the modern. Global awareness and world issues are now on the agenda. For the first time in schools writers from different cultures, such as Ernest Hemingway and Wole Soyinka will be studied. History lessons will teach Islamic studies and pre-colonial India. Pupils in science classes will be made more aware of contemporary topics like genetic engineering and environmental concerns.

lifelearning

life is about learning We have a tendency to believe that as we get older we can no longer learn. That is not so. Research results indicate that we have the capacity to learn at any age. Our learning capacity is like a muscle that needs to be exercised. We are going to need to constantly update our skills in order to keep up with the rapid pace of change.

Learning is not just about the traditional, left-brain, cognitive approach. We have kinesthetic, emotional, spatial, musical and artistic intelligences. Each of these can be developed, opening new directions in our lives. Instead of just limiting education to the young, we want to expand the opportunities so that we can all learn. As we begin to see **LIFE AS A VOYAGE OF LEARNING** we become open to the new. Learning does not have to be a chore, it can be something we want to do. We can all learn so much more about ourselves and the world around us.

what would you like to learn?

ethics

code of honour What are ethics and what role do they play in our lives? Ethics are our character markers. Qualities such as non-violence, consideration, discipline, integrity, patience, simplicity, detachment, appreciation, honesty and compassion, amongst others. We tend to think of ethics as strict moral codes. The should and should nots of religion and society. Barriers that place external restrictions on our behaviour.

Many of us are creating our own ethics and living according to our own internal principles and laws. Our personal ethics evolve from what we have discovered within our own experience of life and spirituality. These personal ethics serve us, they help us develop our personalities. They assist in moving from a self-centred approach to life towards a wider perspective.

We are starting to see a shift towards applying our personal ethics to our whole life. It no longer works to have a different set of ethics dependent on the circumstances. We need to live according to principles that we apply to our life, our business, investment, friendships, partnerships and how we relate to ourselves. What principles do we believe in? What are the qualities that we admire in other people and would like to cultivate ourselves?

Loot, the free advertiser, with offices in London and New York as well as joint ventures in Tokyo and New Delhi, runs a thriving business on the principles of rectitude, honesty, non-discrimination, fairness, community and respect. They reflect the Chairman's personal ethical principles. A culture where half the company's effort goes into producing excellent service and the other half into producing a happy work force. *Loot* is housed in London's most ergonomically advanced offices, providing good ventilation, air and lighting. Four masseuses provide daily massage for those staff working at keyboards. Upward and downward appraisals take place regularly, giving the opportunity not only for management to assess their staff, but also for the staff to assess their management.

divine discontent

seeking Increasingly we are seeking an experience of the sacred. We want to reach beyond the confines of our small, personal world and feel the presence of a greater life that gives us meaning and sustenance. This search is deeply embedded in our consciousness. Historically, religion has provided culture with institutions through which we could experience the sacred.

Religions have not embraced the challenges of the future and no longer provide the answers for the modern seeker. We need new beliefs, new formats, new buildings: a new language.

a regeneration

The more science discovers about how the world works, the more God recedes. We used to view God as the great force of creation, but now we are realizing that we can create according to our own wants. Mystery is no longer needed in religion, so much more can now be explained. We used to pray for healing, but now we trust doctors and focus that faith and expectation on them. IVF means children are no longer gifts from God. Therefore a search is on to find a deeper, more spiritual form of religion, that acknowledges the progress of science and addresses our current existential needs.

the individual seeker

Many of us are forming our own beliefs, synthesizing the old and the new, the Eastern and the Western traditions. We are looking for a new mysticism beyond the walls of the temple. Discovering our own personal mythologies and investigating transpersonal psychology. In time we will develop institutions to support our explorations.

new formats

Whilst there are fundamentalist reactions to change, contemporary religion is in the process of developing. New movements are researching, pooling traditions. Buddhists are talking to Muslims, Christians to Jews. Small groups are taking responsibility with lay leaders, discovering new avenues of spiritual inspiration. Looking at the roots of these traditions to examine what is valuable, and combining ideas to move forward and discover a new, meaningful religion. Religion will have to look within to find how it wants to be expressed in the new millennium. People are rediscovering rich esoteric traditions: alchemy, the Kabbalah, Sufism and Paganism are re-emerging from centuries of hiding.

spiritualy it is a time of great chaos and also of great opportunity

oneplanet

the global village We can get on a plane and within a day be practically anywhere on the planet. We can pick up a mobile phone from a café in Paris to call a friend in the most isolated region of Siberia. At a touch of our computer keyboard we can surf an electronic wave of bytes that can take us across the globe. Who has the power and influence in this process of making a global village?

It used to be the governments of the large industrial nations. But today it is the multi-national corporations that are increasingly gaining influence over the world economies.

eastwestnorthsouth

We are in the process of **CULTURAL BLENDING.** An interchange of ideas, practices, philosophies, technologies and art. We can eat Japanese sushi, read translations of Persian poetry, practice Indian yoga and wear American trainers. In our urban centres we are being exposed to a new world. We are learning more about cultures and global traditions and what they can offer our lives.

think global, act local

Whilst this process of internationalization is going on, we are still living our normal lives. In our daily lives, small is beautiful. We relate to our local area, the environment, people and place. To increase our appreciation of life we need to invest our time in the local sphere. This is where our lives happen, where the stories that we live unfold. It is important for all of us to develop the roots of community. A village takes time to build, and the present sociological trends have led us towards separation, not community. We cannot form a global whole without caring for the local community, our families and ourselves. It is increasingly important that we keep our roots, that we remember our local traditions, folklore and customs. These form the fabric of our communities which might otherwise be lost in an homogenized global culture. Take the time to learn a little more about our local area, its history, mythology, environment. How can each of us support the local? We need to be able to hold both the whole and the particular, to live a local life and know that we form part of a larger, planetary family.

go glocal!

conclusion

I have taken you on a journey exploring many aspects of our lives. In examining the essence of the various topics, it becomes obvious that there are common ingredients to a **recipe for the future.**

this recipe is:

ease, sensuality, integrity, simplicity, authenticity, quality, meaningfulness, naturalness, reassurance, time efficiency, protection, individuality, purity, internationality and comfort.

A mix of these qualities affects everything from cosmetics to education. New developments and thinking in one field often influence other fields.

alternative becomes mainstream

From politics to health, food, energy, relationships, spending, art, spirituality and education.

alternative has come of age

It is shedding its niche image and becoming an accepted option. Both the **ALTERNATIVE AND MAINSTREAM ARE NOW UNFOLDING IN PARALLEL.** This can be seen from the development of local currencies to the Euro, organic food to nutriceuticals, clanning to net-chat rooming, and holistic health to genetic research.

our challenge is to fuse these opposites

They can work together. We are also seeing a polarity develop between the **MICRO** and the **MACRO.** For example: atomic energy to solar energy, local thinking to global thinking, personal health to the health of the planet.

can we expand our vision and live our lives in a way that encompasses both?

The new developments of our society evolve away from the comfortable mainstream. Research scientists, artists and mystics offer us new knowledge, understanding and wisdom. It takes time for the mainstream to accept these visionaries and to allow our perceptions to change. We all have a tendency to stay within the known. It gives us a sense of security. The mindscape of the mainstream is behind the times.

we need to catch up

There are many questions to be asked, answers to search for and changes to be made. We need to prepare for the future. Change is an opportunity. We can make it work for ourselves. We will need new skills and understanding. I hope that this book has developed some awareness of the possibilities of the future, stimulated your imagination, encouraged and supported you in

mindscaping
the
future

what we are today comes

from our thoughts of yesterday

and our present thoughts

build our life of tomorrow

Siddartha Gautama

for further information contact:

mindscaping@compuserve.com

www.Mindscaping.com

suggested reading

Most of the information in this book has been accumulated over years of discussion, reading and research. Instead of listing every book (many of which I no longer remember) I have selected books I have found particularly valuable.

ourselves

Spirit of the Home,
Jane Alexander, Thorsons, 1998
Voluntary Simplicity,
Duane Elgin, Quill, 1993
The Undiscovered Self,
Carl Gustav Jung, Routledge, 1958
Living Your Dying,
Stanley Keleman, Random House, 1974
On Death and Dying,
Elizabeth Kubler-Ross, Routledge, 1970
The Chi Kung Way,
James MacRitchie, Thorsons, 1997

The Musical Life,
W.A. Mathieu, Shambhala, 1994
Care of the Soul,
Thomas Moore, HarperPerennial, 1992
Anatomy of Spirit,
Caroline Myss, Random House, 1997
A Whack on the Side of the Head,
Roger Von Oech, Thorsons, 1983
Music and the Mind,
Anthony Storr, Ballantine, 1992
The Book of Yoga,
Sivananda Yoga Centre, Ebury Press, 1983
Feng Shui made Easy,
William Spear, Harper Collins, 1995
The Origin of Everyday Moods,
Robert Thayer, Oxford, 1996
Journey of the Heart,
John Welwood, HarperPerennial, 1996

ourwork

Tips for Time Travellers,
Pete Cochrane, Orion Business Books, 1998
Wisdom at Work,
Let Davidson, Larson Publications, 1998
The Good Life,
Demos Collection, Demos, 1998
The Hungry Spirit,
Charles Handy, Arrow Books, 1997
The Corporate Mystic,
Gay Hendricks & Kate Ludeman,
Bantam Trade, 1996
Business@ The Speed of Thought,
Bill Gates, Penguin, 1999
Next,
Ira Matathia & Martan Salzman, HarperCollins, 1997
Money and the Meaning of Life,
Jacob Needleman, Currency/Doubleday, 1994
On the Cards,
Perri6 & Ivan Briscoe, Demos, 1996
The New Business Paradigm,
Michael Ray & Alan Rinzler, Tarcher/Putnam, 1993
The Dance of Change,
Peter Senge, Nicholas Brealey Publishing, 1999

oursociety

7 Kinds of Smart,
Thomas Armstrong, Plume, 1993

Learning Beyond the Classroom,
Tom Bentley, Routledge, 1998

The Turning Point,
Fritjof Capra, Bantam Doubleday
Dell Publishing, 1998

Stop Ageing Now,
Jean Carper, HarperPerennial, 1996

Ageless Wisdom, Timeless Mind,
Deepak Chopra, Rider Books, 1993

History of the Future,
Peter Lorrie & Sidd Murray-Clark, Doubleday, 1989

Path of Parenting,
Vimala McClure, New World Library, 1999

Healing with Whole Foods,
Paul Pichford, North Atlantic Books, 1993

The Rebirth of Nature,
Rupert Sheldrake, Park Street Press, 1991

Birth of a Mother,
Daniel Stern et al., Basic Books, 1999

Tao & Dharma,
Robert Svoboda & Arnie Lade, Lotus Press, 1995

The Secret Life of the Unborn Child,
Thomas Verny & John Kelly, DTP, 1981

index

A

abroad, living/working 180–1
achievement, assessment 193
advertising 112
age and ageing 145–7
age-appropriate learning 190
AIDS 69
allopathic medicine 158–9
alternative paradigm 210–11
annual hours 95
architecture, energetic 29, 97,172
art 133–5
Austin, Prof James H. 129
awareness 17, 127–9

B

balance 38
banking, ethical 119–20
bio language 124
Bio-Regional Development Trust 176
birth 83–5
bodywork 158
brain, psychotechnology 168
branding 107–11
British Airways 98
buildings, environment-friendly 176–7
bulk-buying 116

C

car boot sales 116
career breaks 94–5
cashless society 117
charity shops 116
chi 28
choice 17, 145, 152
cities 179
clanning 35
co-operation 51
Co-operative Bank 120
communication 123–5
communities:
 global village 205–7
 new paradigm 179–81
complementary medicine 157–61
computers, human-centred 166
Conde Nast 177
connections 19–20, 31–5
conscious death 86
constitution 155
consumer goods, marketing 109–12, 153
consumers:
 ethical 105–8
 as individuals 101–3
continuing education 62, 64, 75–7, 195–6
cosmetics 72–3
craft goods 176
cultural blending 206
curiosity 75–7
currency, global 121
cutting edge thinking 16
cyber language 125

D,E

death 83–4, 86–7
DIY 64
drinks 151–5
e-cash 118, 119
Earth Day 139
EasyJet 107
eco-optimism 142
education 62, 64, 75–7, 189–96
elders 146–7
electronic wallets 117, 118
EMU 121
energetic architecture 29, 97, 172
energy 25–30
energy (fuel) 166–7
English 123–5
environment 141–3
ethics:
 and banking 119–20
 and consumers 105–8
 and investments 47
personal 197–9
exercise 43–4
Exeter University 159
experiences 62

F

families 34–5, 183–7
farmers' markets 115
fashion 71–2
feng shui 29–30, 97, 172
festivals 139
finance 45–7, 117–21
flea markets 116
flexi-homes 174
flexi-time 95
food 56, 63, 151–5
freetime 61–5
funerals, DIY 87

G,H

gardening 63, 172
gay relationships 33
gender 79–81
gene mapping 159
global village 205–7
habitat 171–7
health 41–4, 53-6
hearing 53, 55
holidays 64
holistic medicine 157–61
home, working from 95
home births 85
Home Electronic System 174
homes 63–4, 171–7
household support teams 97
hot desking 94

I,J

imagineering 128
immune system 42–3, 152
individuality:
 as a consumer 101–3
 expressing 71–3
information:
 accessible 77
 boom, and technology 163–5
 and marketing 111–12
information technology 98–9
Integrated Medical Centre 161
integration 19–21
internet 64
 artistic tradition on 134–5

on-line investments 119
on-line shopping 113–14
intranet 98
investments, on-line 119
Itsu restaurant 108
job sharing 94
Jurlique 73

L
language, English 123–5
learners, needs 192
learning, lifelong 62, 64, 75–7, 195–6
local exchange trading systems (lets) 120
location 13
Loot 199
Losal, Lama Yeshe 129

M
mail-order shopping 116
maintenance 173
marketing 109–12, 153
marriage 33
medicine 29, 41–2, 157v61
meditation 129
meeting points 63
men, and gender 79–81
micro/macro fusion 211
migration, social 179–81
mindscape, definition 11–13
mindset 15, 19, 21, 128, 212
M.I.T., Boston 166
Miyajima, Tatsuo 135
money 45–7, 117–21
Motor Development International 167
music 134–5

N
nanotechnology 167
National Curriculum 193
nature, and ecology 141–3
neighbourhood learning centres 191
New Ways to Work 96
nutriceuticals 154
nutrition 151–5

O
on-line investments 119
on-line shopping 113–14
organic produce 151–4
out-sourcing 50

P
parenting 185–7
Peabody Trust 176
Phillips 174
Planet Organic 154
population 183–4
portfolio of jobs 91
Positive Parenting 186
prana 28
privacy 149–50
products, marketing 109–12
protection 149–50
psychotechnology 168

Q
qi 28
quality 59, 175

R
relationships 31–5, 69
religion 137–8, 201–4
Revive Time project 135
right, being 17
rituals, contemporary 137–9
routines 15
rural living 180

S
sacred, search for 201–4
safespending 47
Samye Ling Tibetan Centre 129
saving 47
security 149–50
Seimens 174
self care 37–9
senses, healing dynamics 53–6
sexuality 67–9
sharing:
jobs 94
time and talents 51
Shell 129
shopping 113–16
sight 53, 54
simplicity, voluntary 57–9
smart cards 118
smell 53, 54
soul 65
spending 45–6
super foods 154
support teams 97

T
taste 53, 56
team working 93
technology 98–9, 107, 163–9, 175
term-time working 94
thinking, creative 17, 127–9
time 49–51, 57
touch 53, 55
traditions, contemporary 137–9
trends 16–17

U,V
Unilever 111
Urban Splash 173
v-time 95
vehicles, ZP (zero pollution) 167
virtual reality 165
virtual working 93
voice recognition technology 165

W
wallets, electronic 117, 118
water 152
women, and gender 7981
work, future structure 47, 91–9
workplace, design 97–8

Y, Z
yourself, expressing 71–3
Zen 129
Zero Energy housing development 176

Stephanie Churchill was born in the Netherlands and was educated in France, Germany and the UK. In 1970 she came to live in England and started *Stephanie Churchill PR,* a public relations consultancy specializing in the development and repositioning of brands. She has given lectures throughout Europe on Mindscaping and her background encompasses design, retail management, journalism and manufacturing. She lives in London and loves exploring the wild parts of the world. She has three grown up children.